BLANK FOR BLEEDS

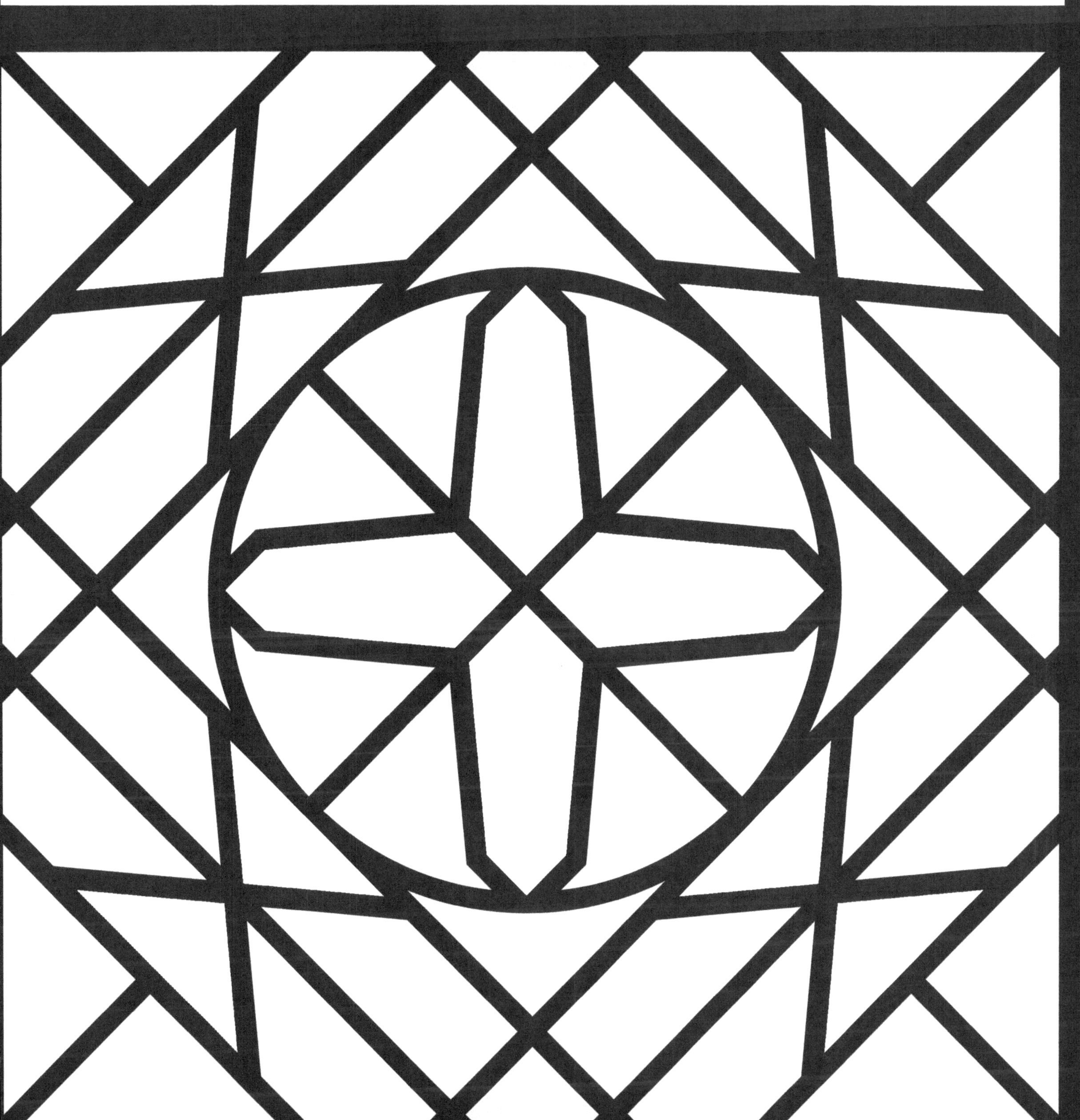

BLANK FOR BLEEDS

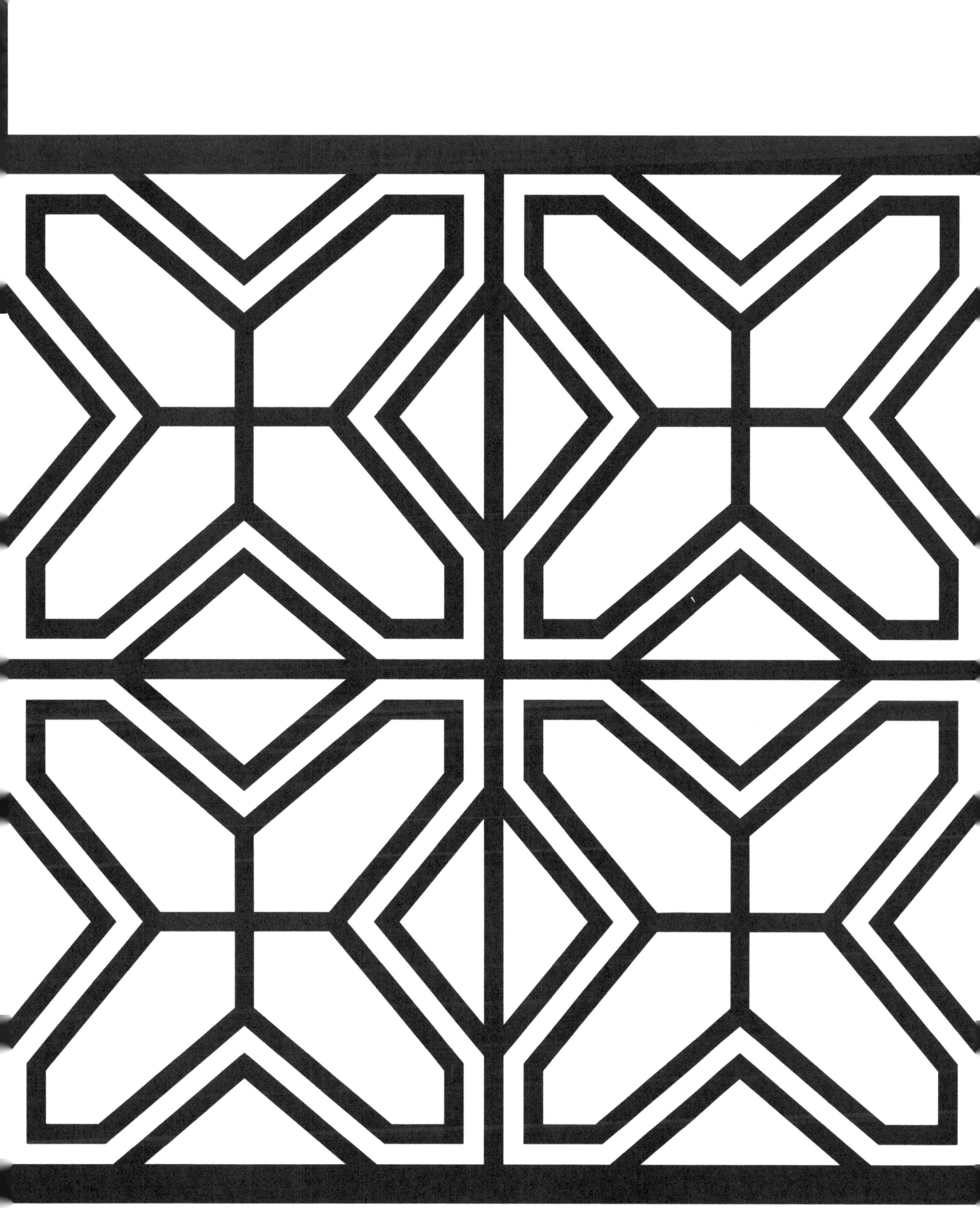

BLANK FOR BLEEDS

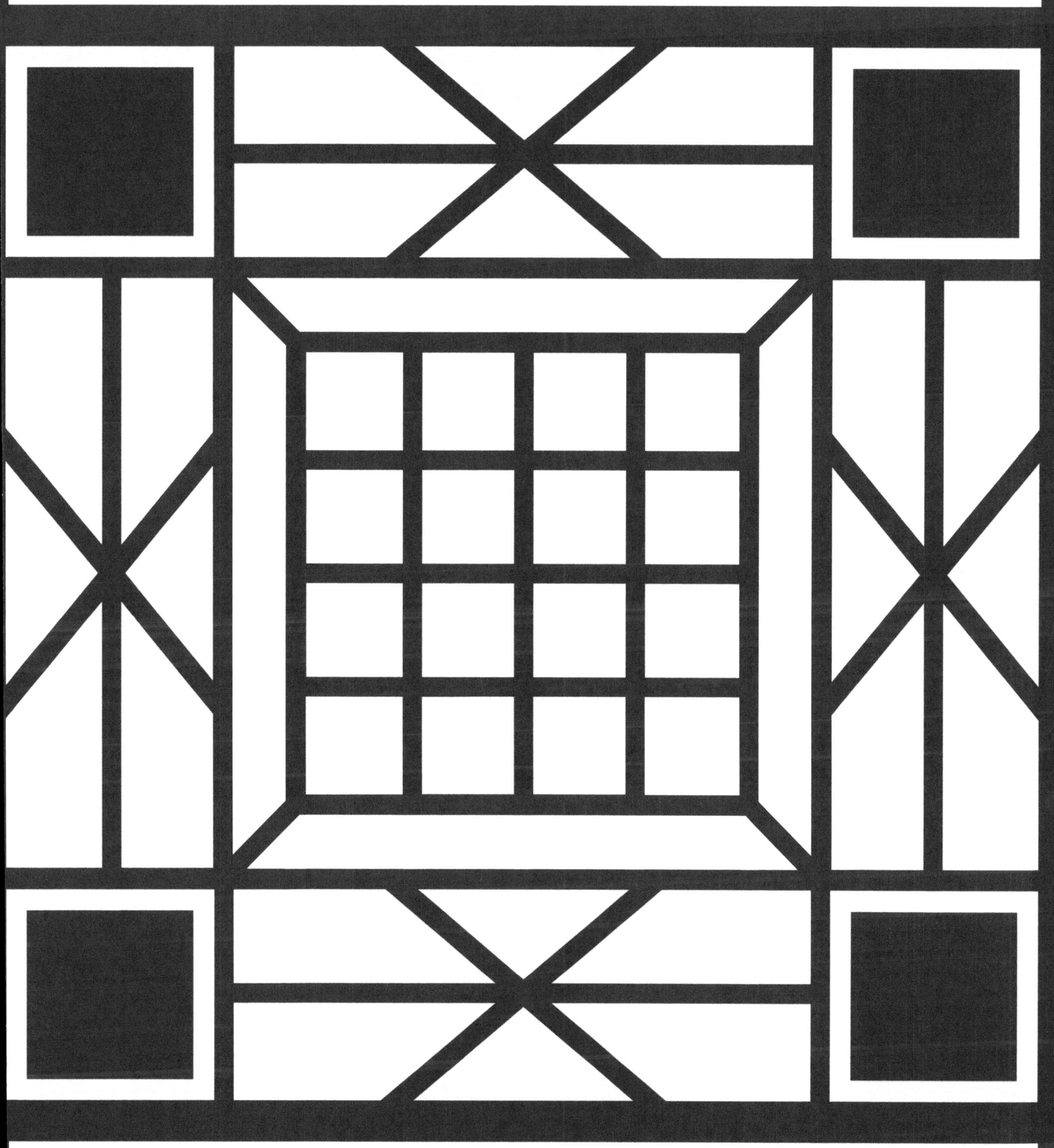

BLANK FOR BLEEDS

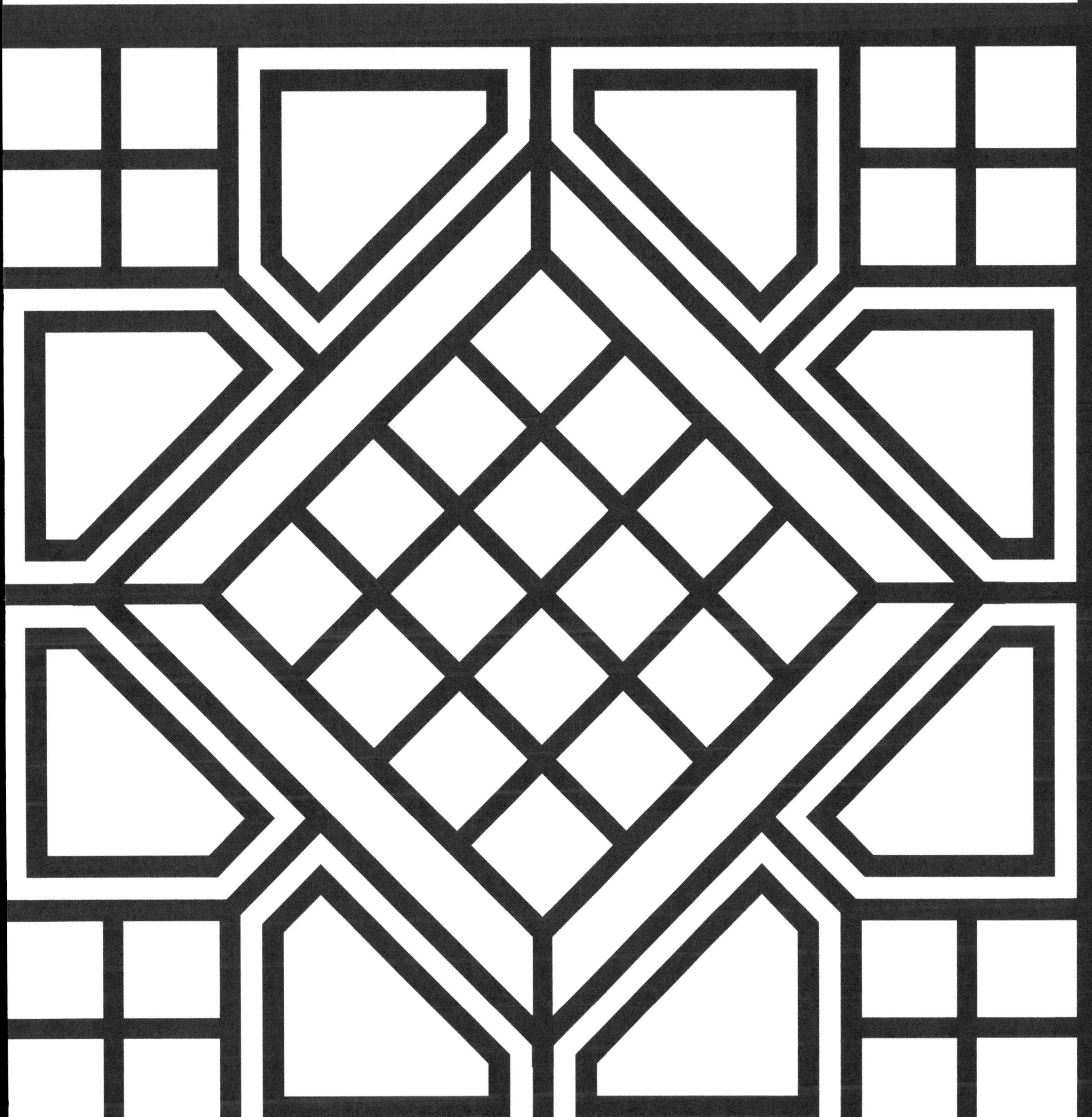

BLANK FOR BLEEDS

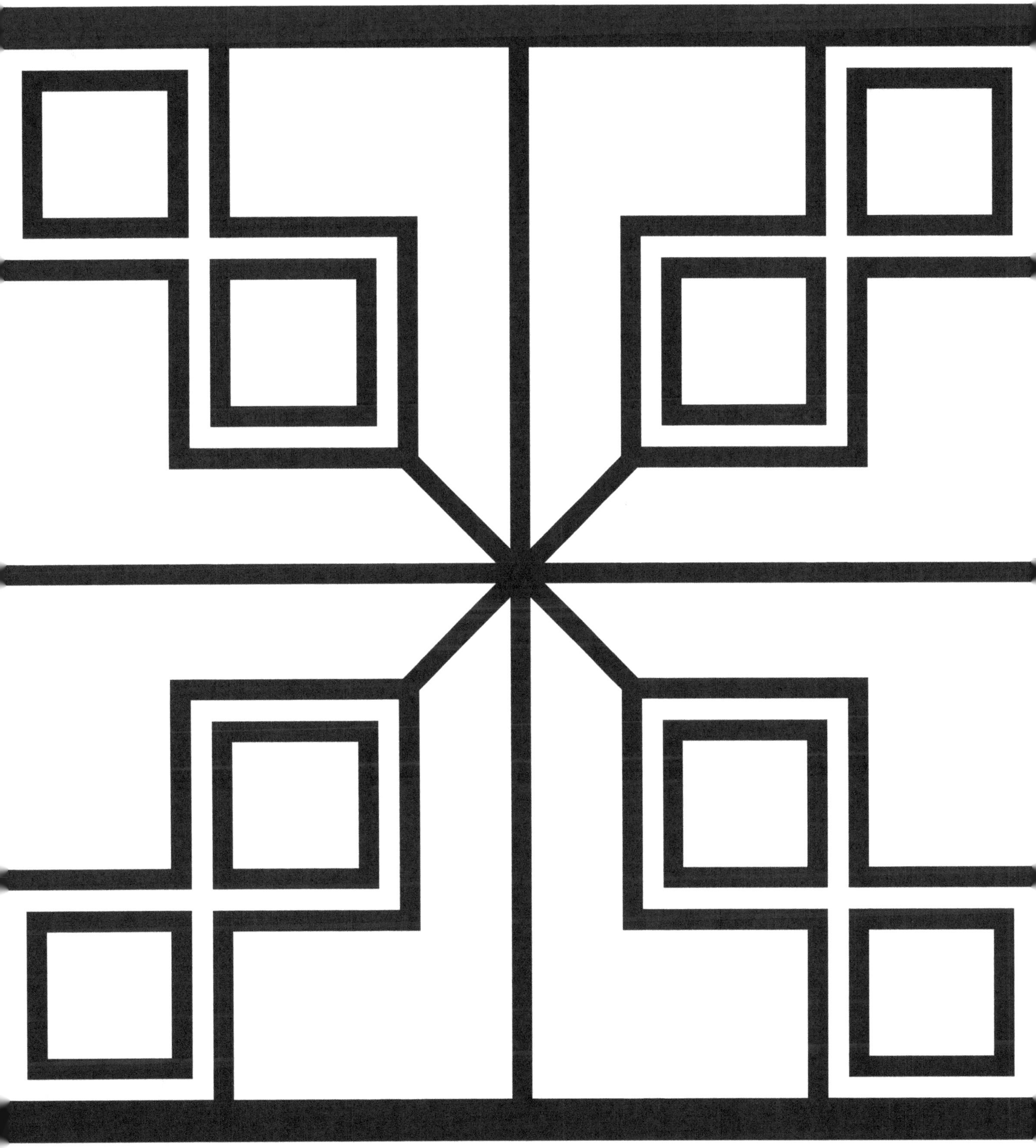

BLANK FOR BLEEDS

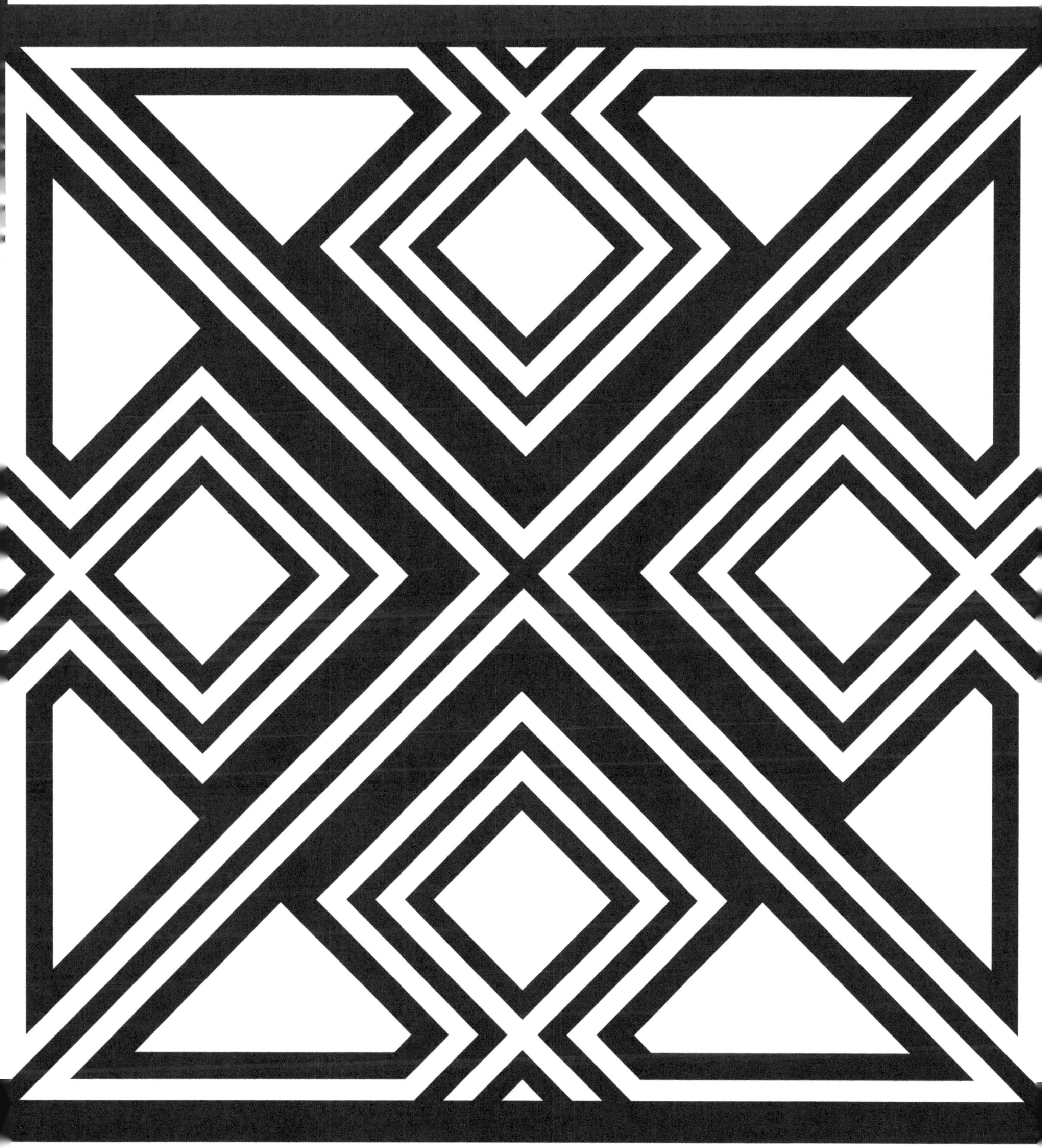

BLANK FOR BLEEDS

BLANK FOR BLEEDS

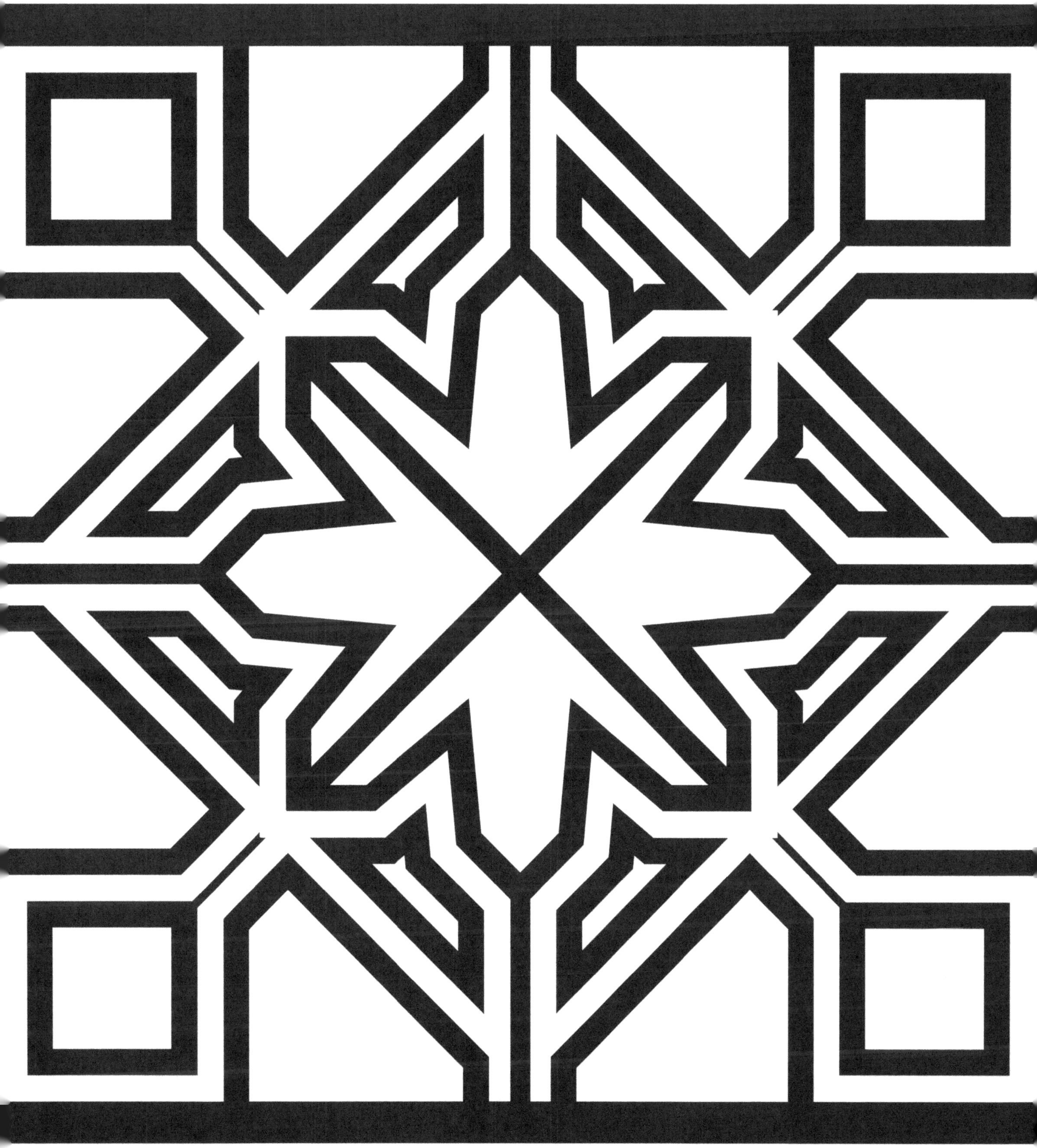

BLANK FOR BLEEDS

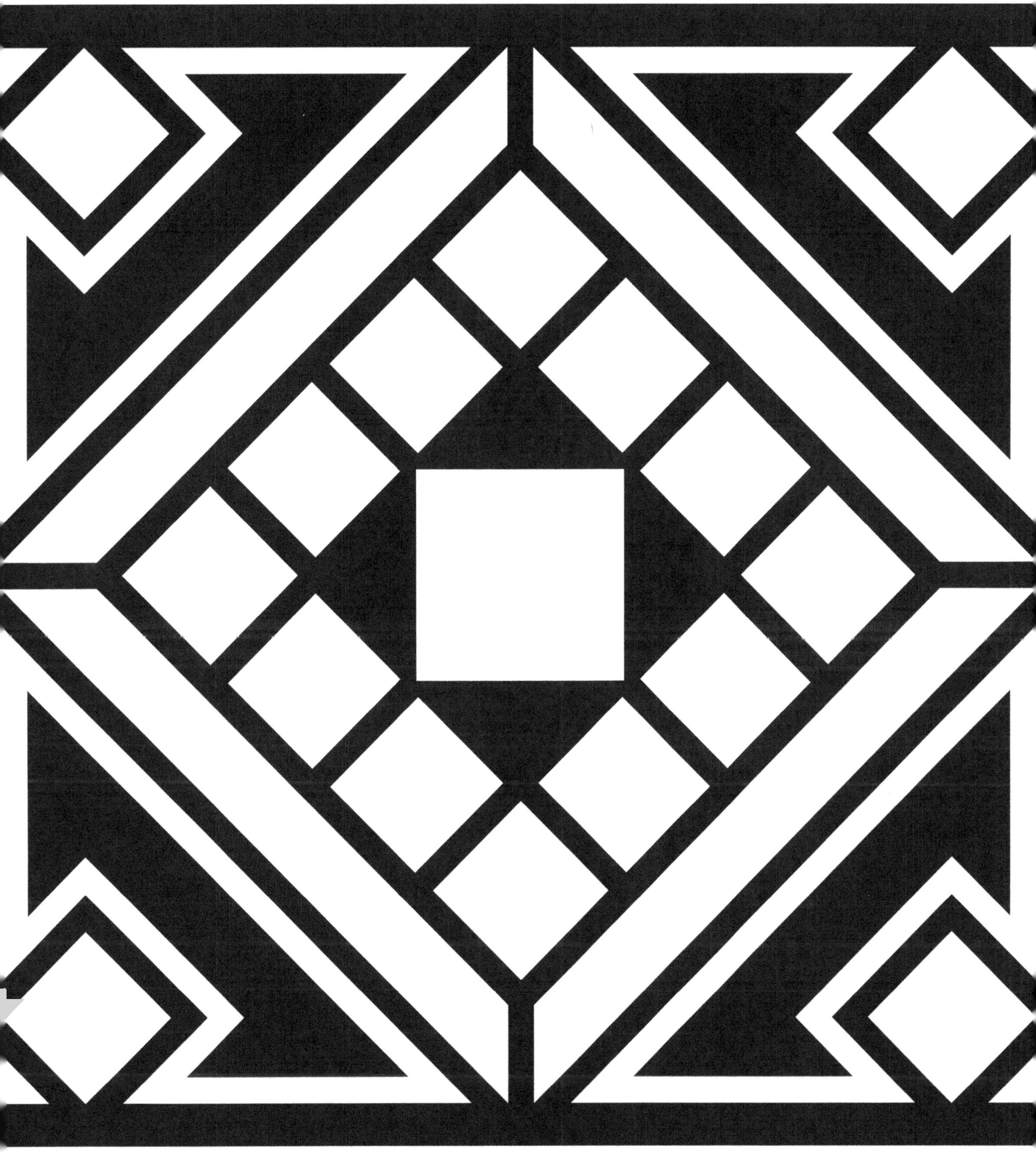

BLANK FOR BLEEDS

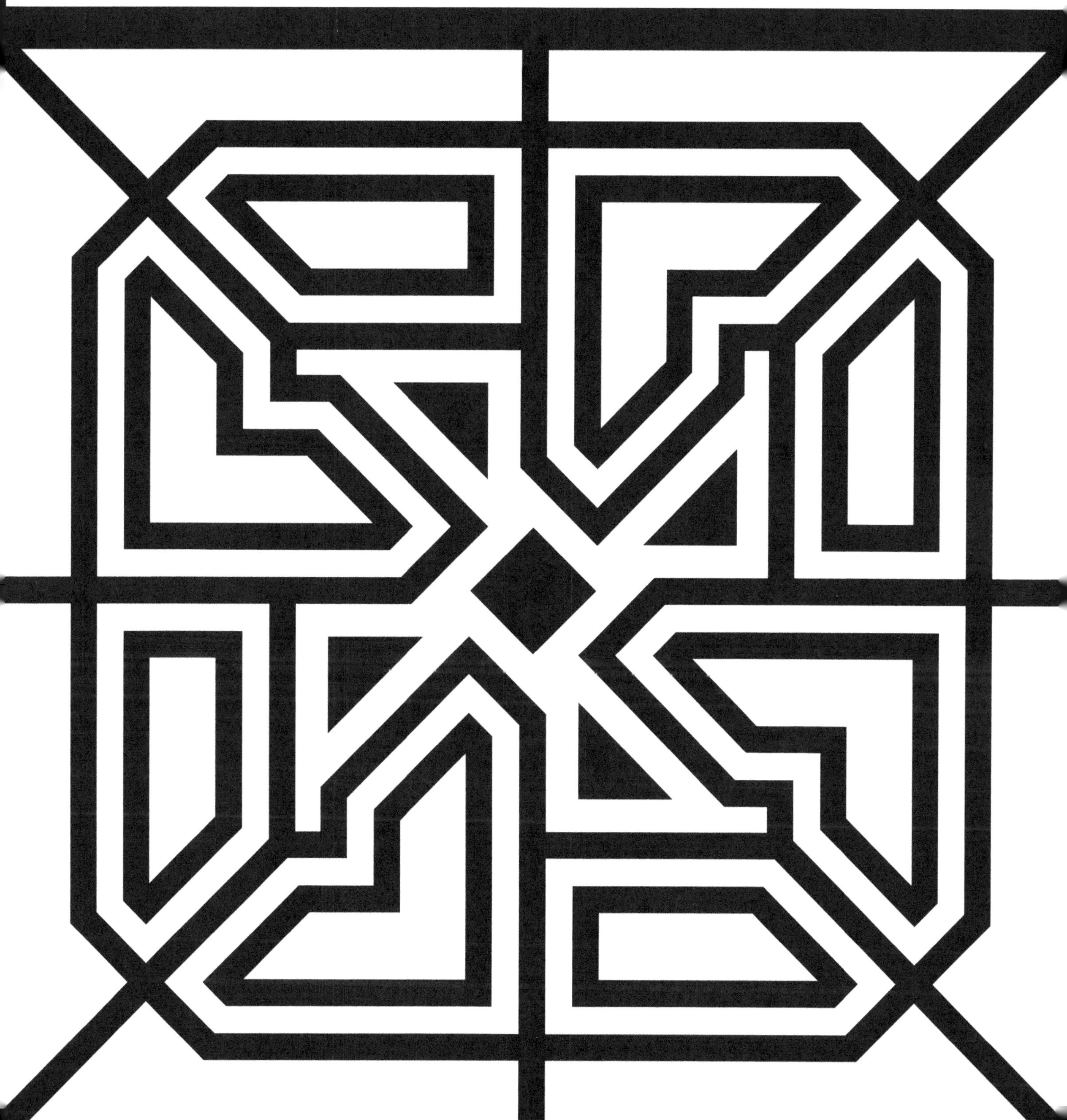

BLANK FOR BLEEDS

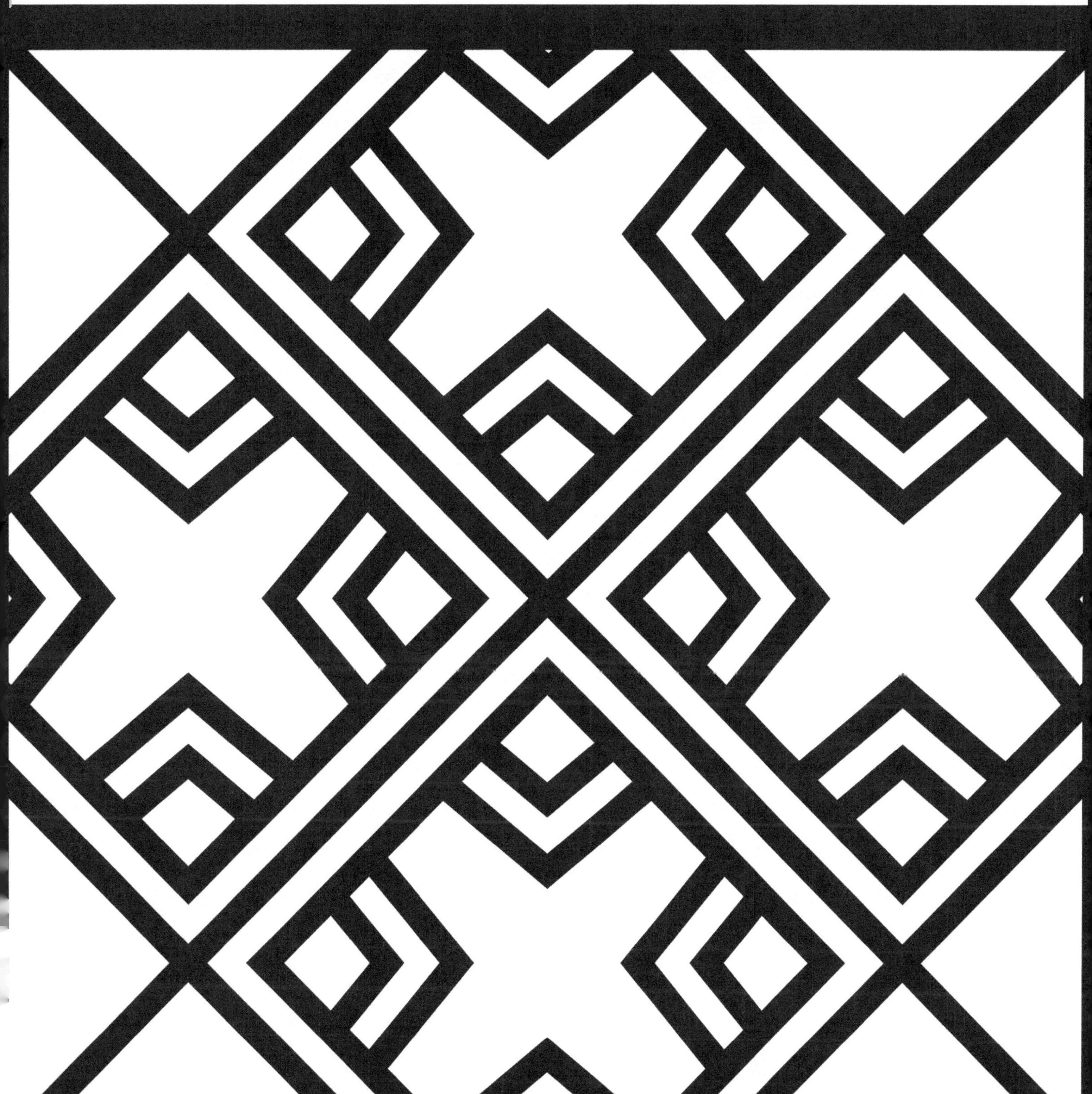

BLANK FOR BLEEDS

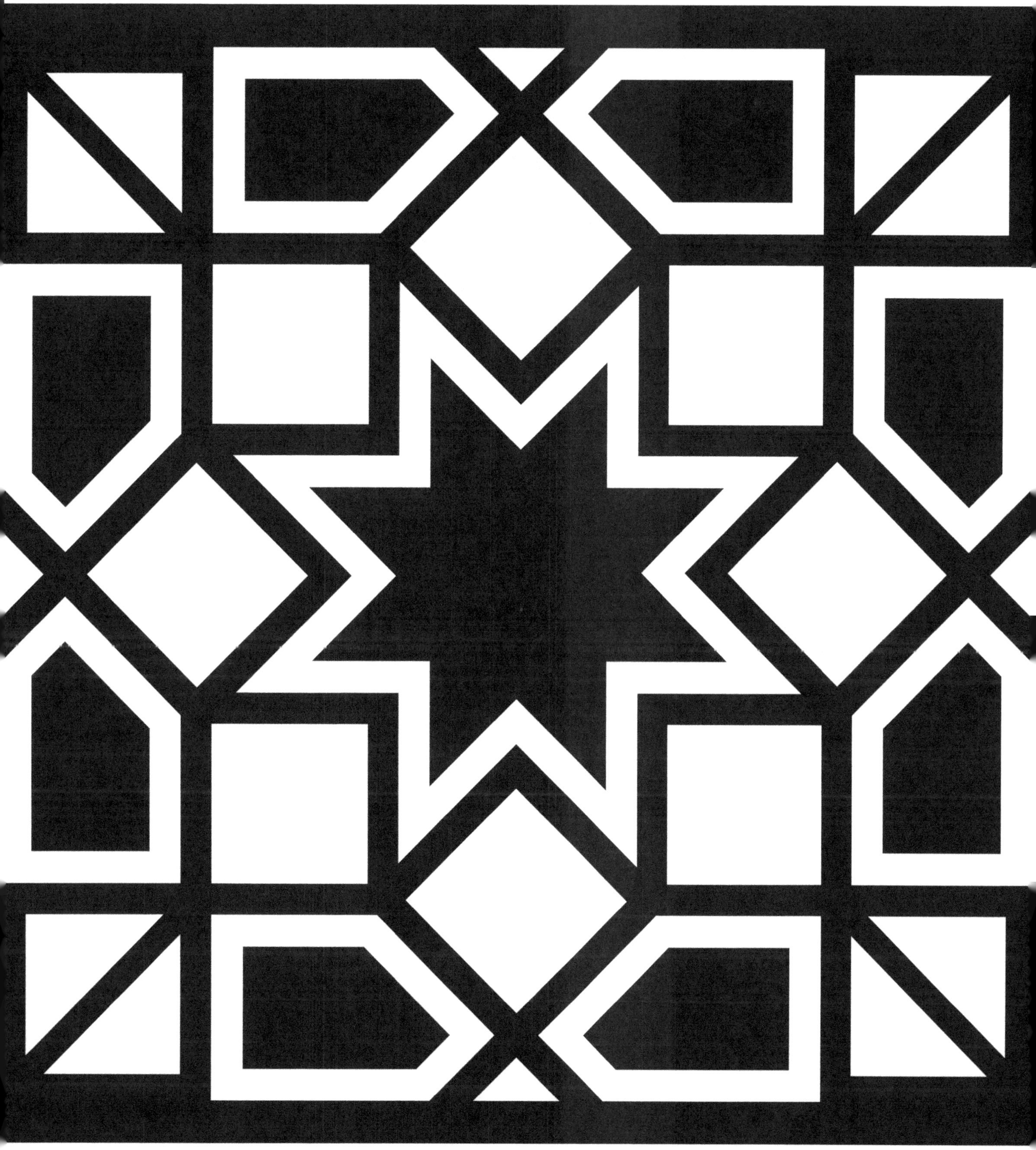

BLANK FOR BLEEDS

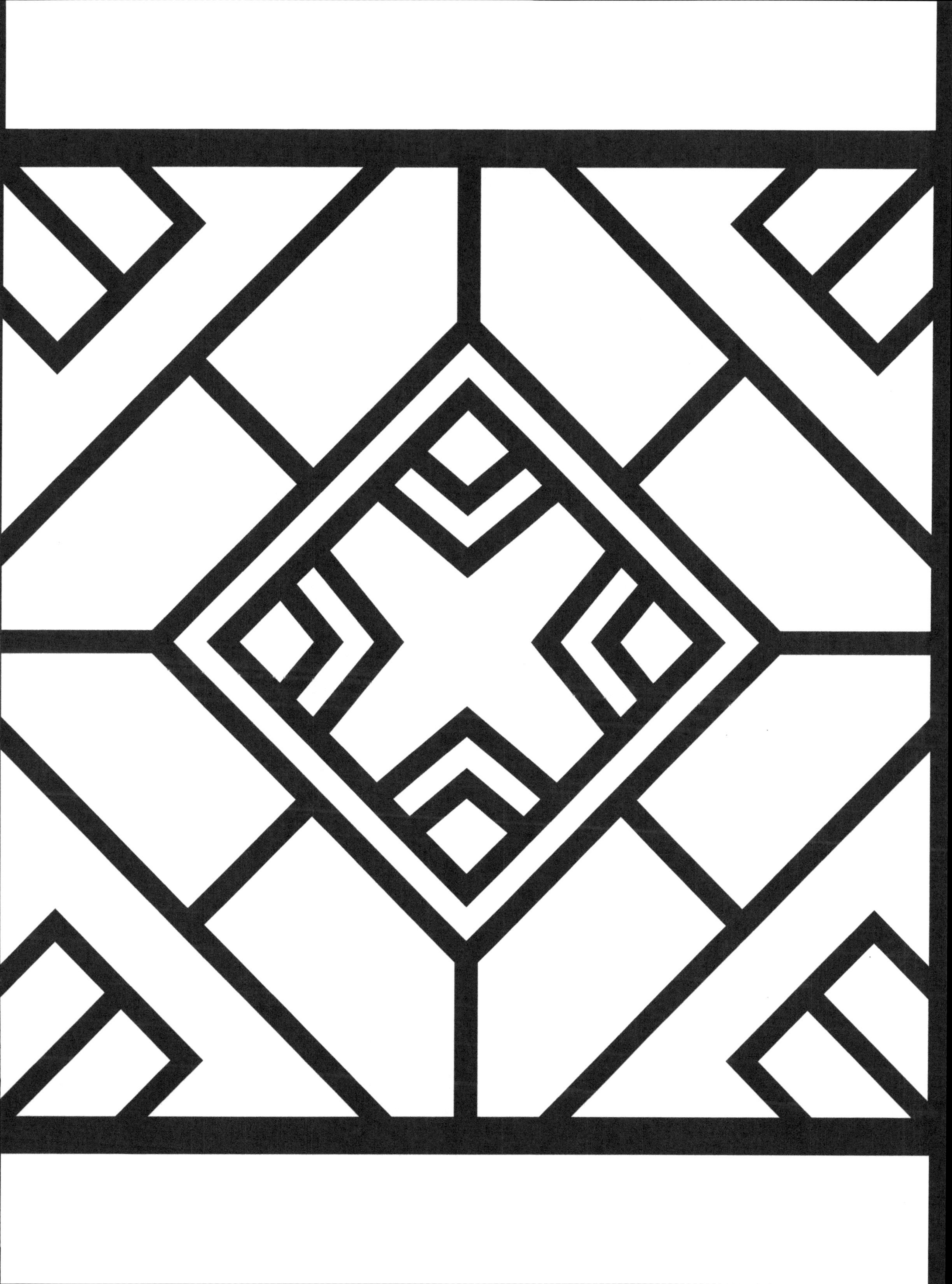

BLANK FOR BLEEDS

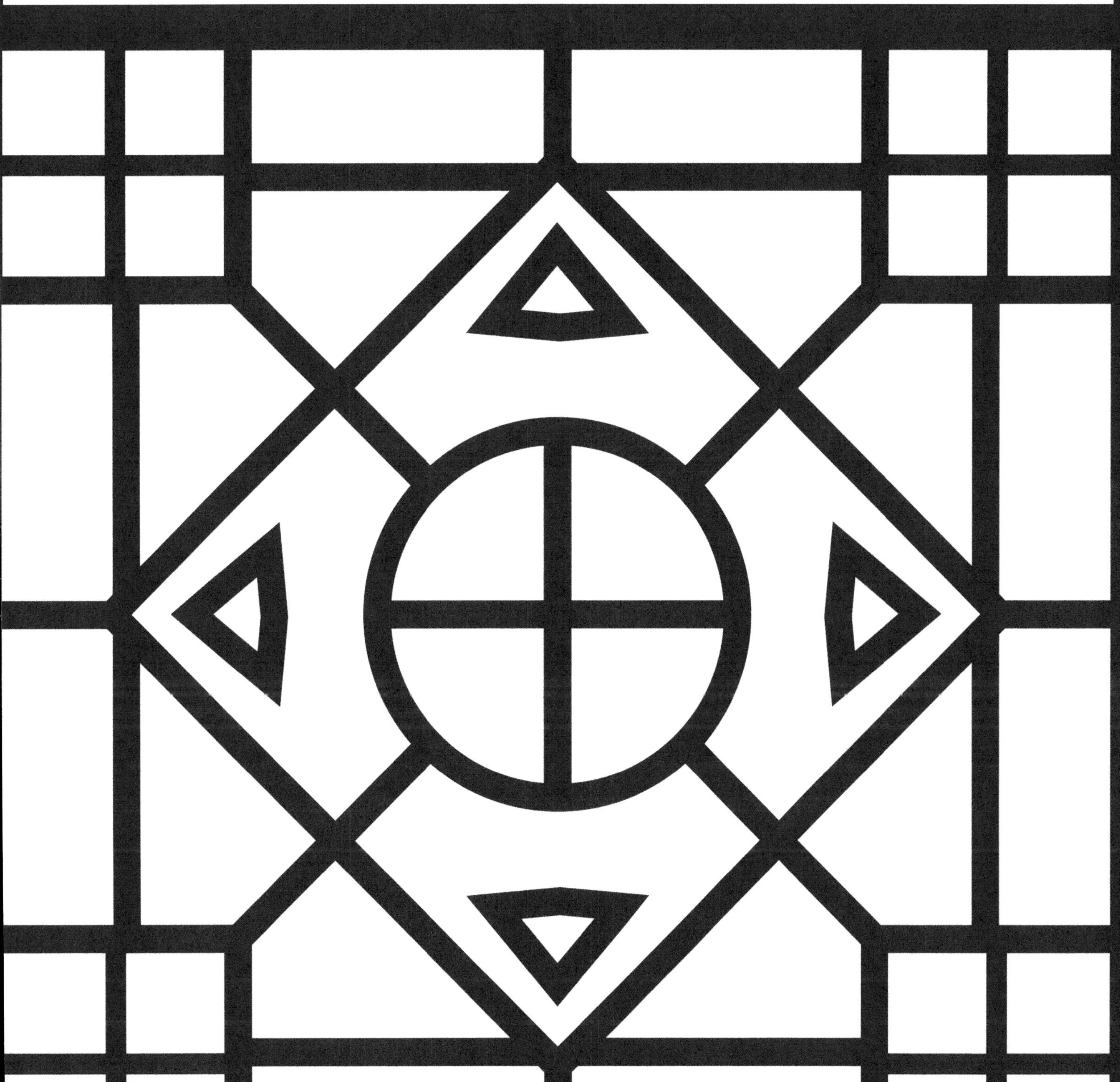

BLANK FOR BLEEDS

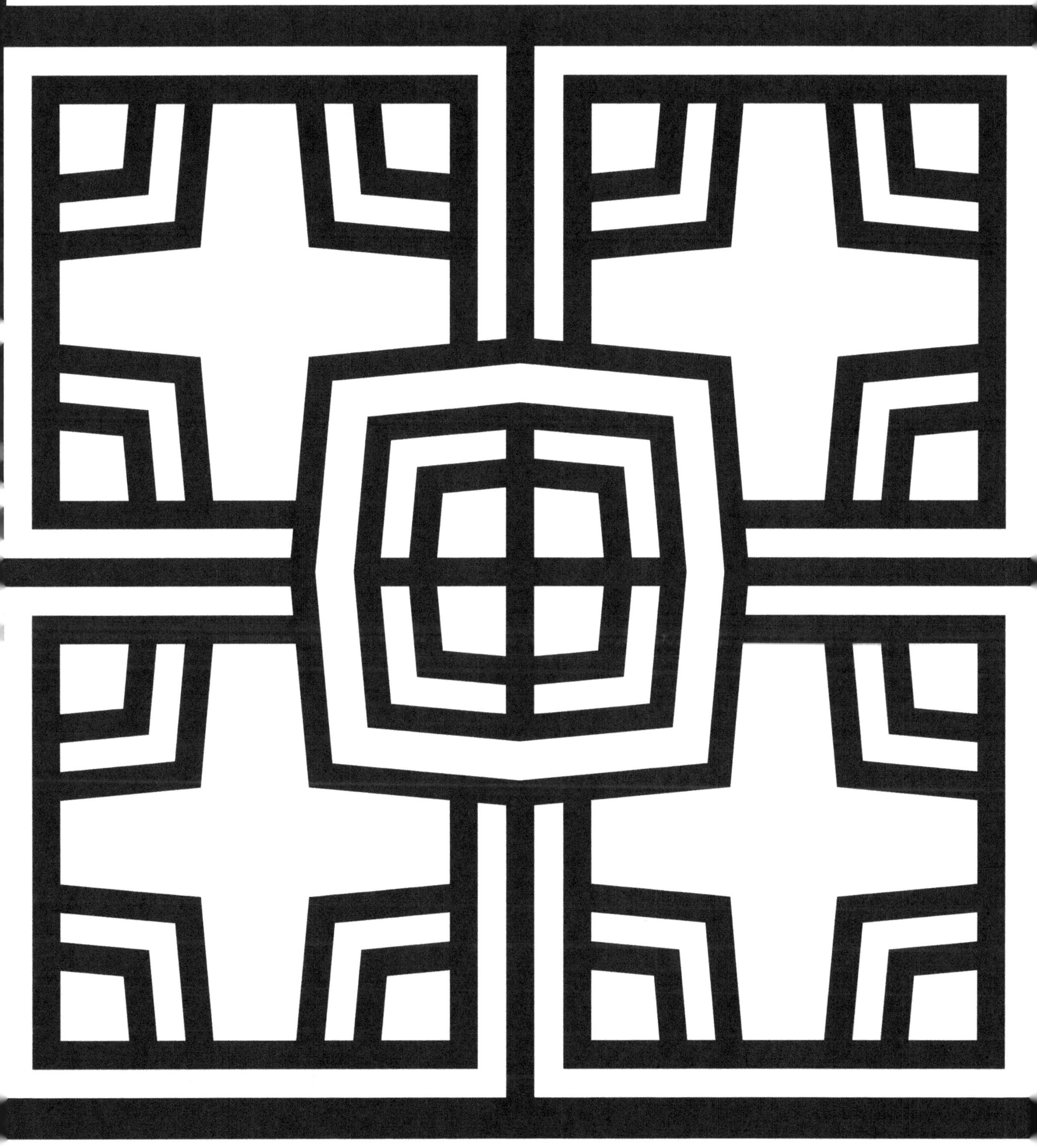

BLANK FOR BLEEDS

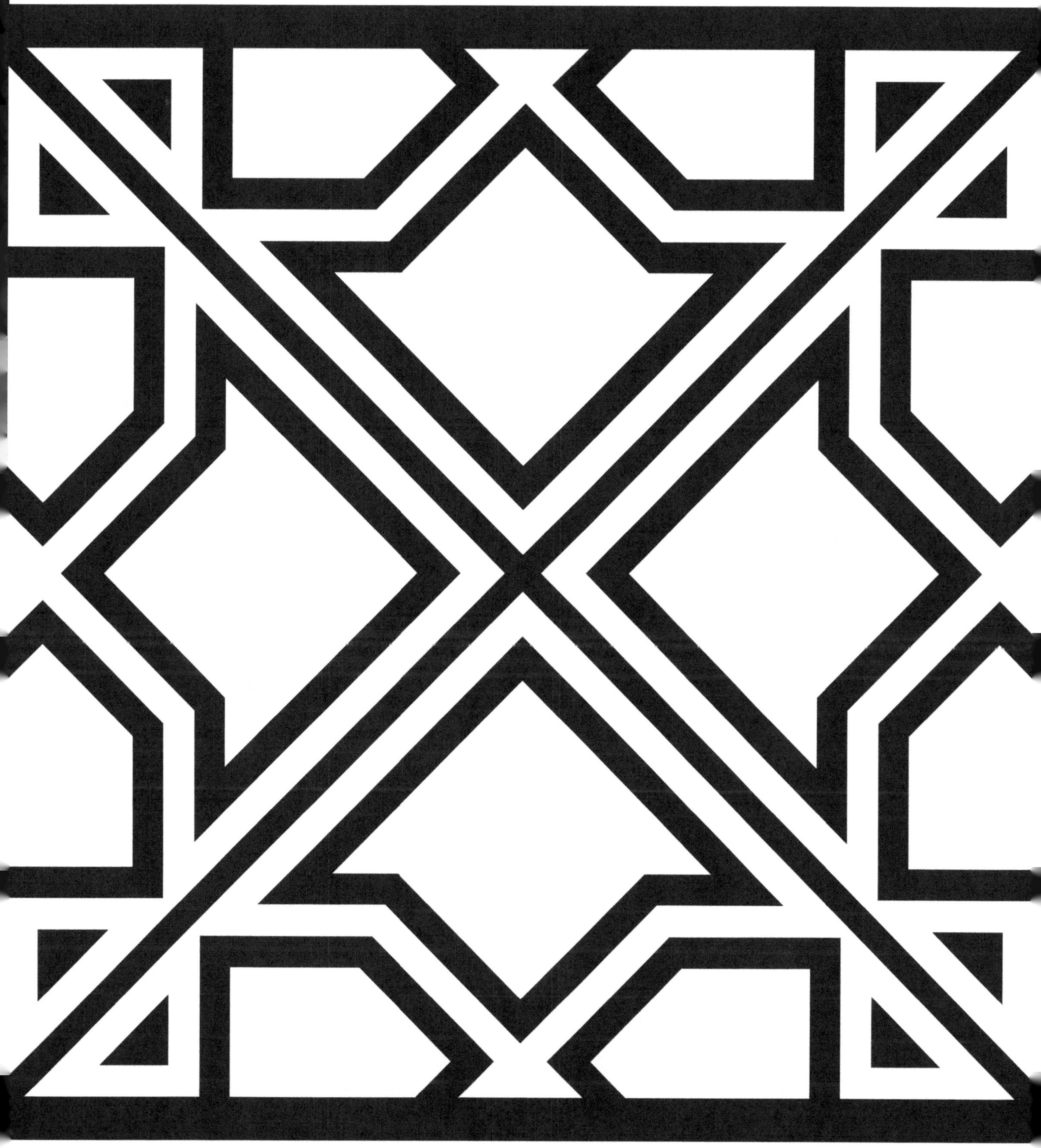

BLANK FOR BLEEDS

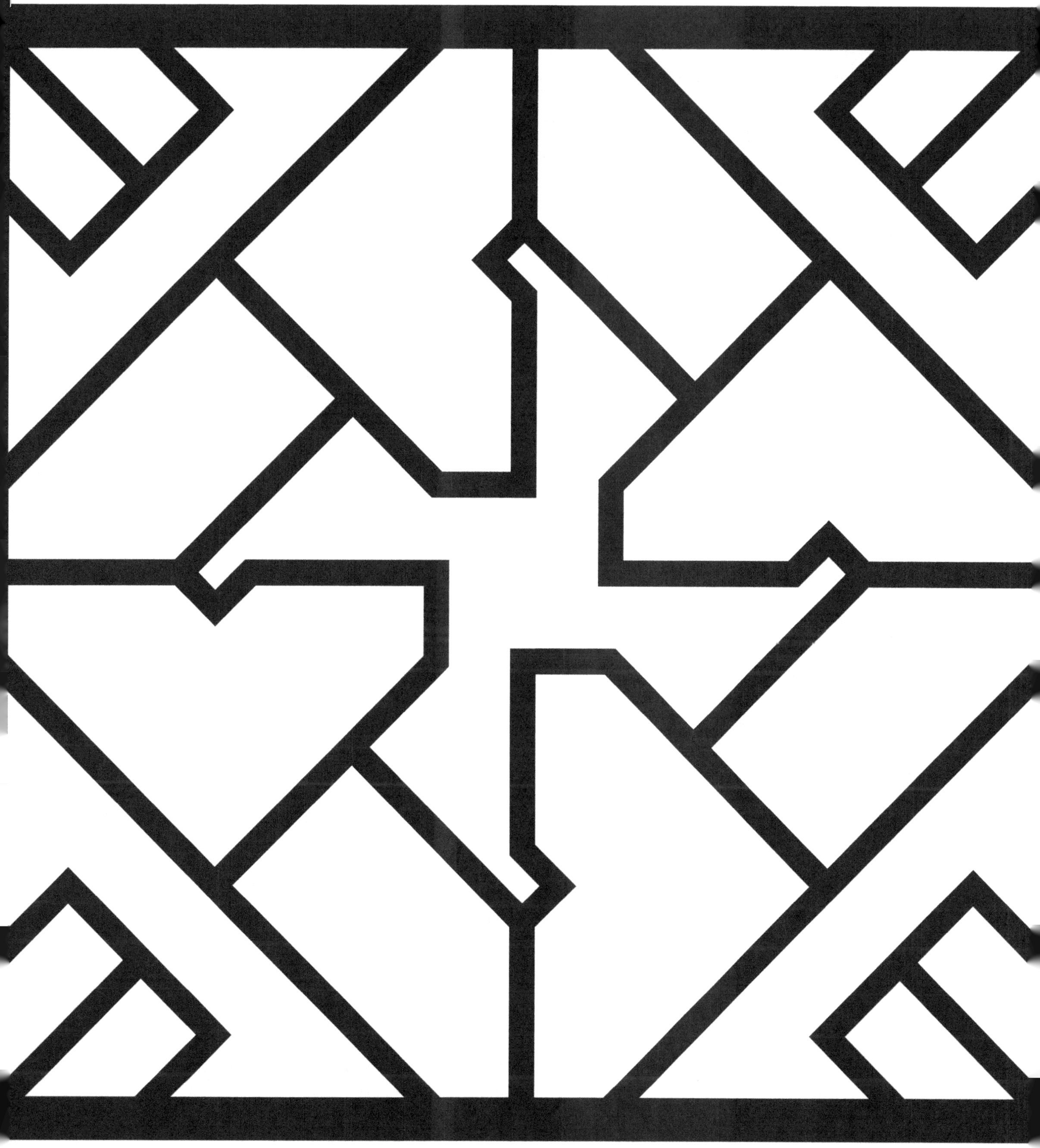

BLANK FOR BLEEDS

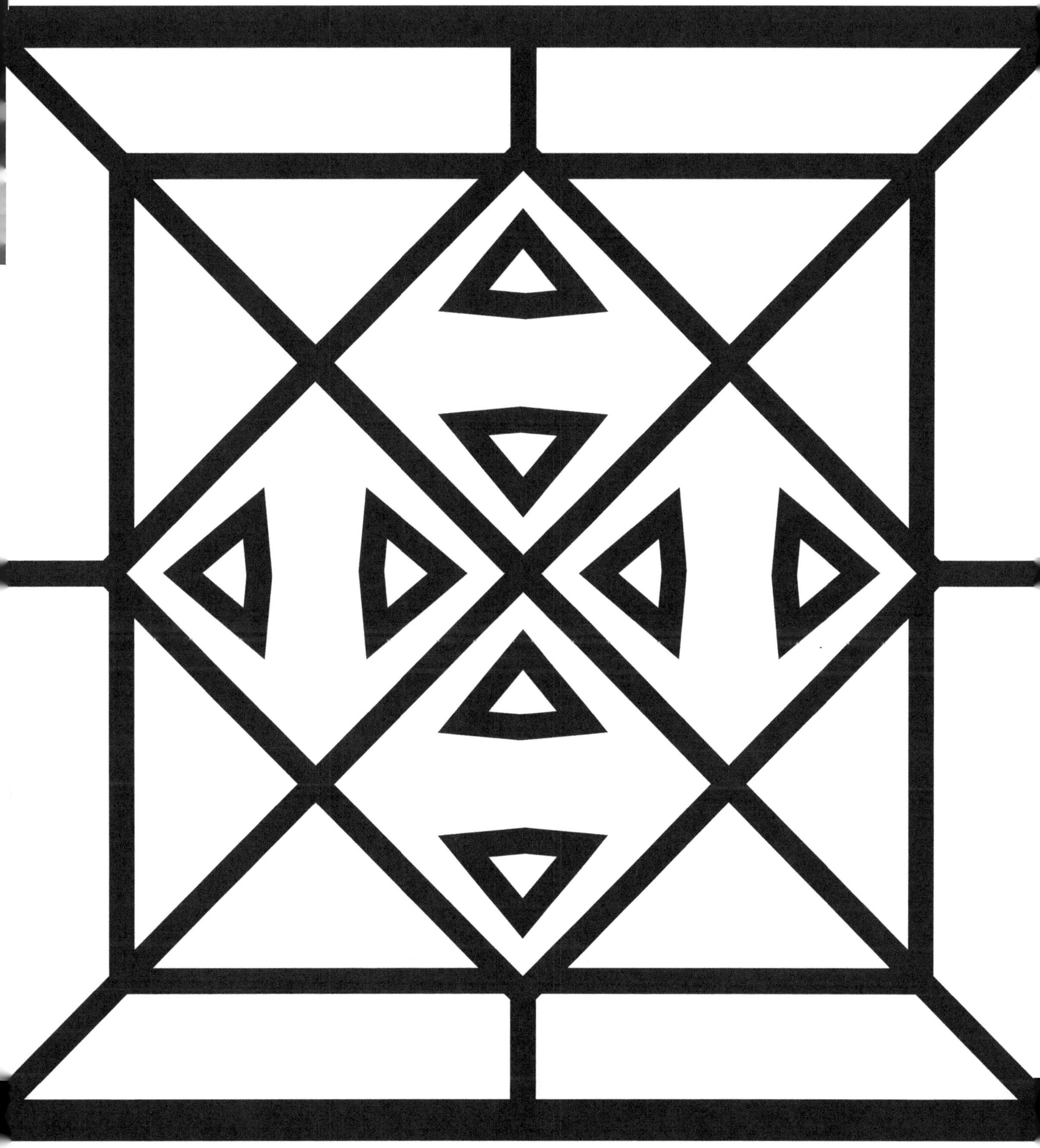

BLANK FOR BLEEDS

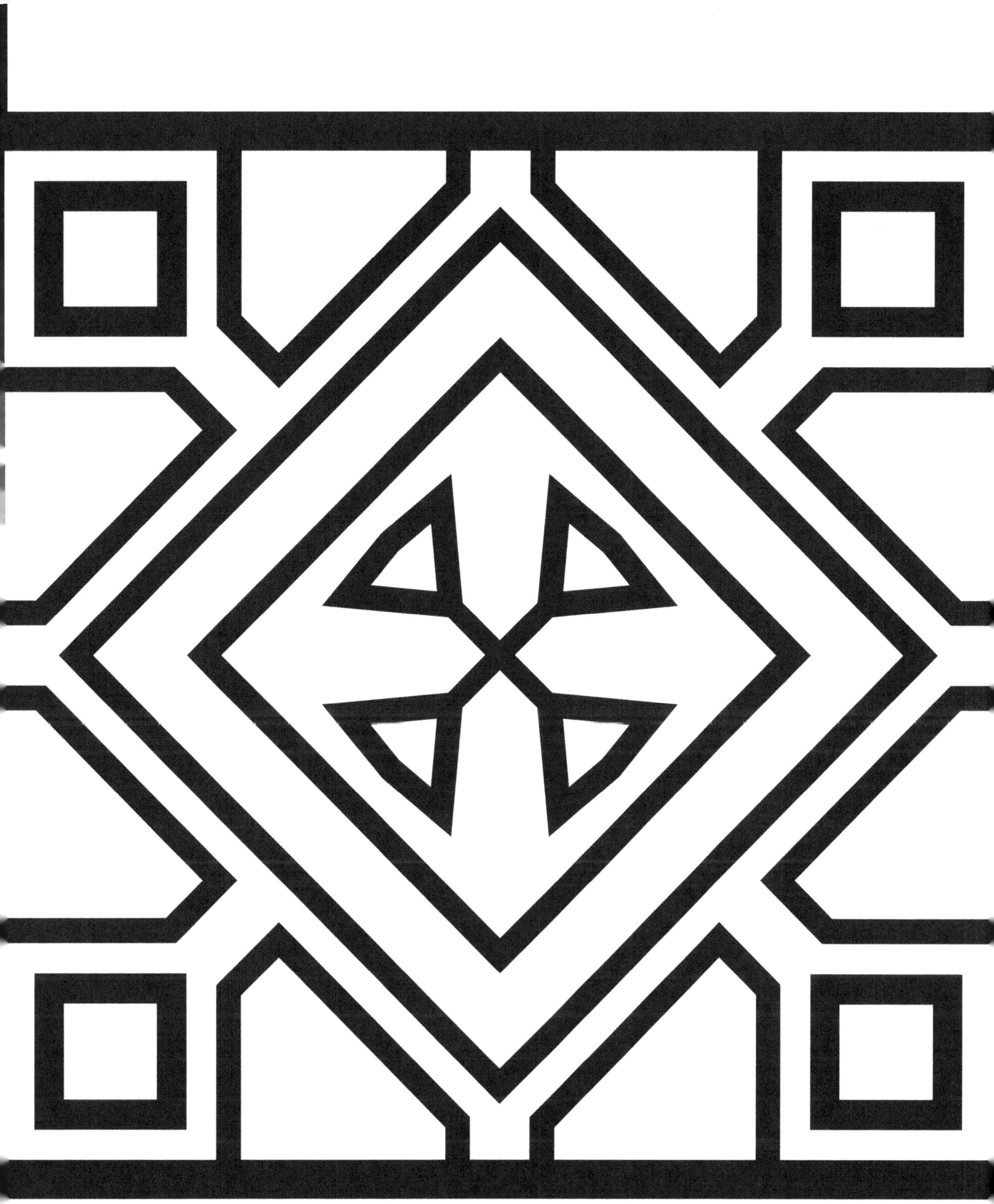

BLANK FOR BLEEDS

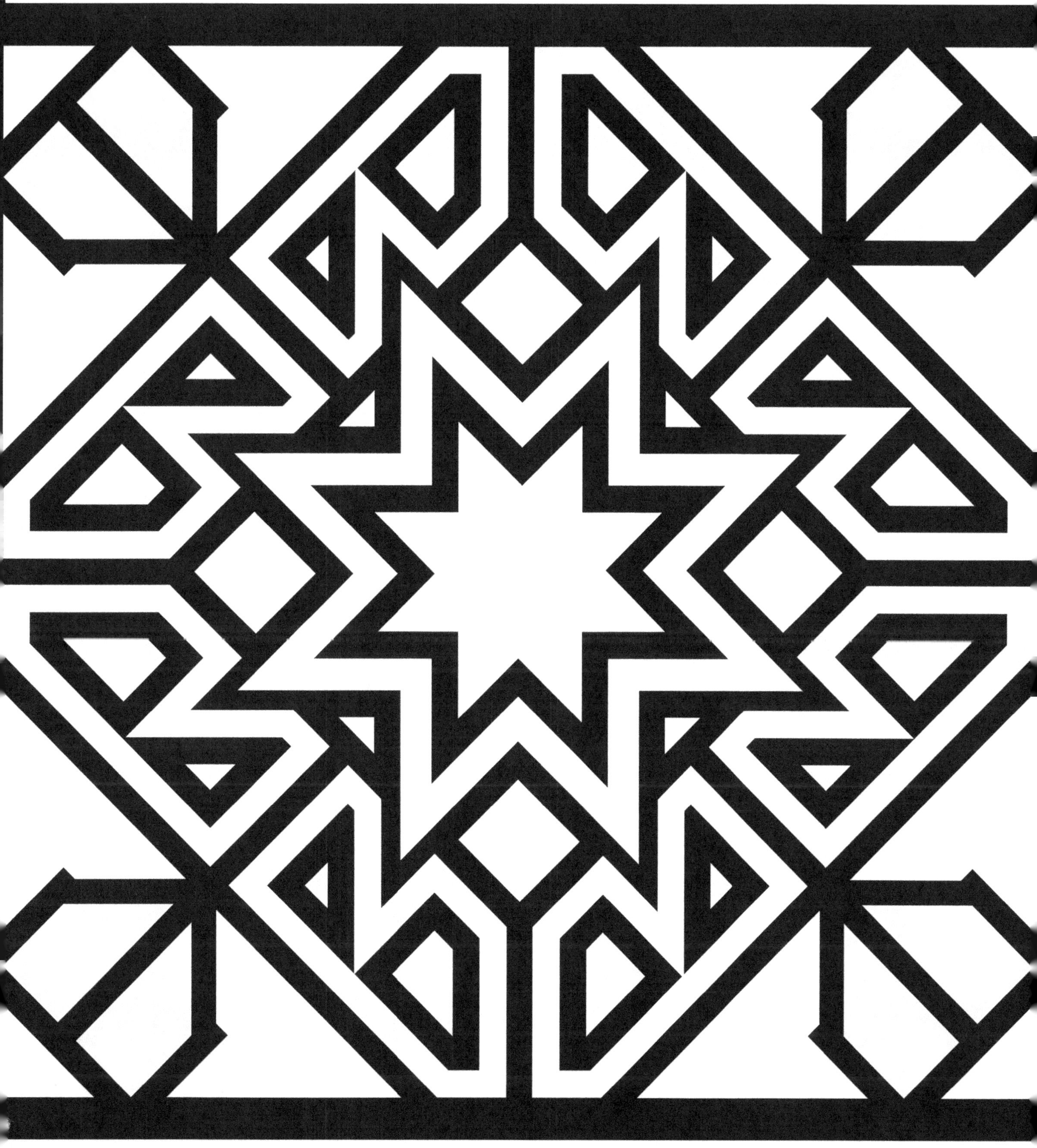

BLANK FOR BLEEDS

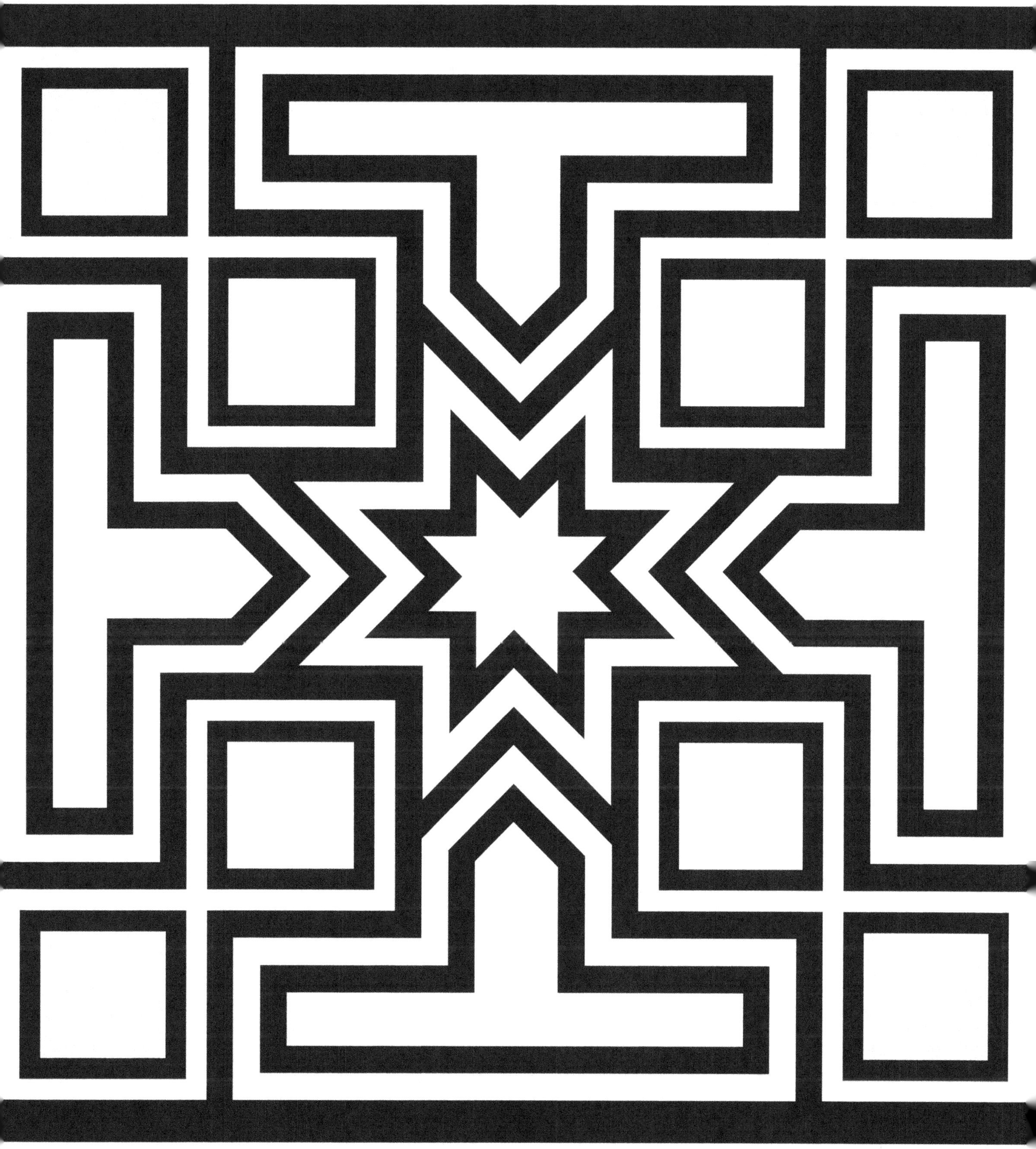

BLANK FOR BLEEDS

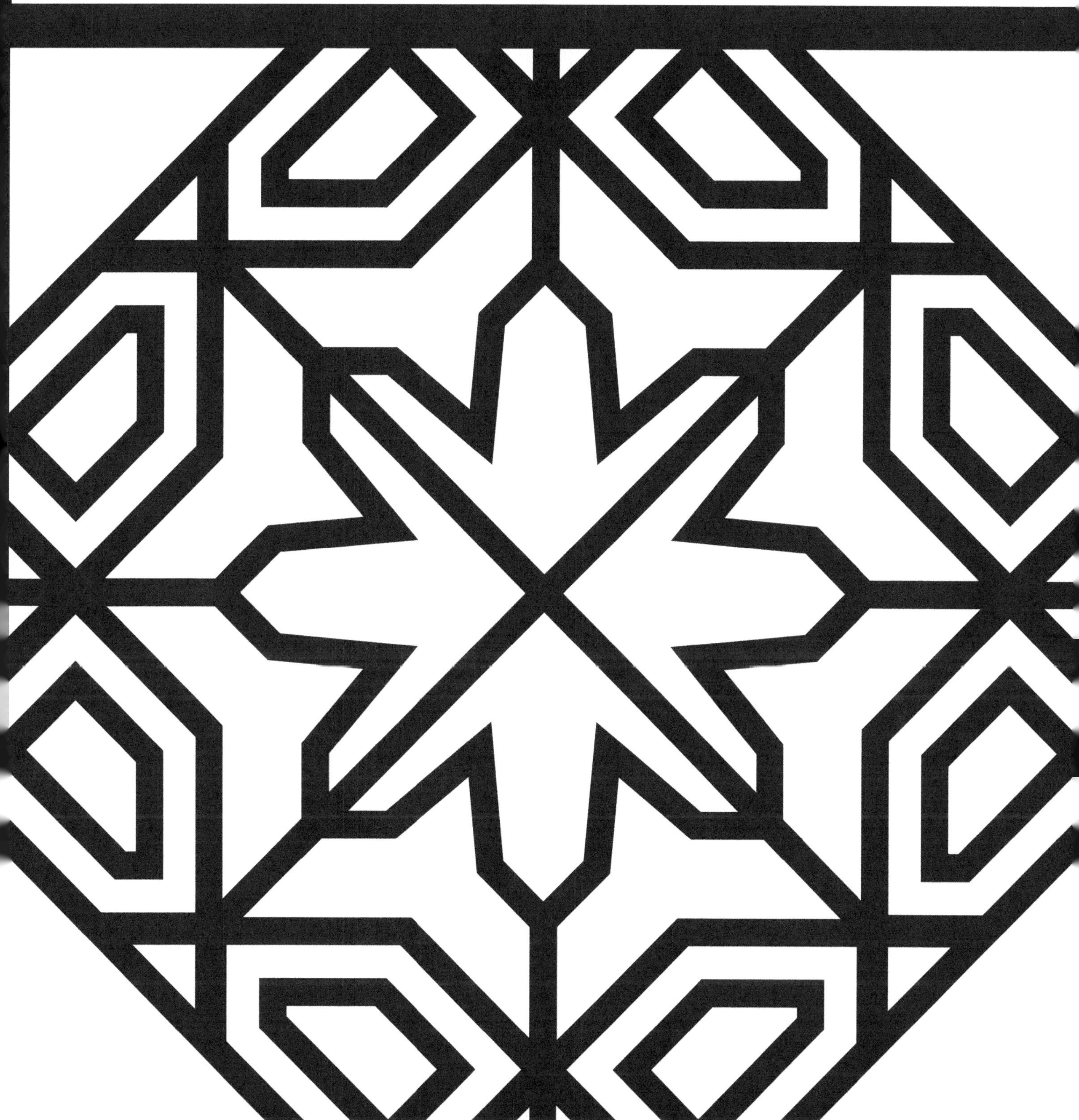

BLANK FOR BLEEDS

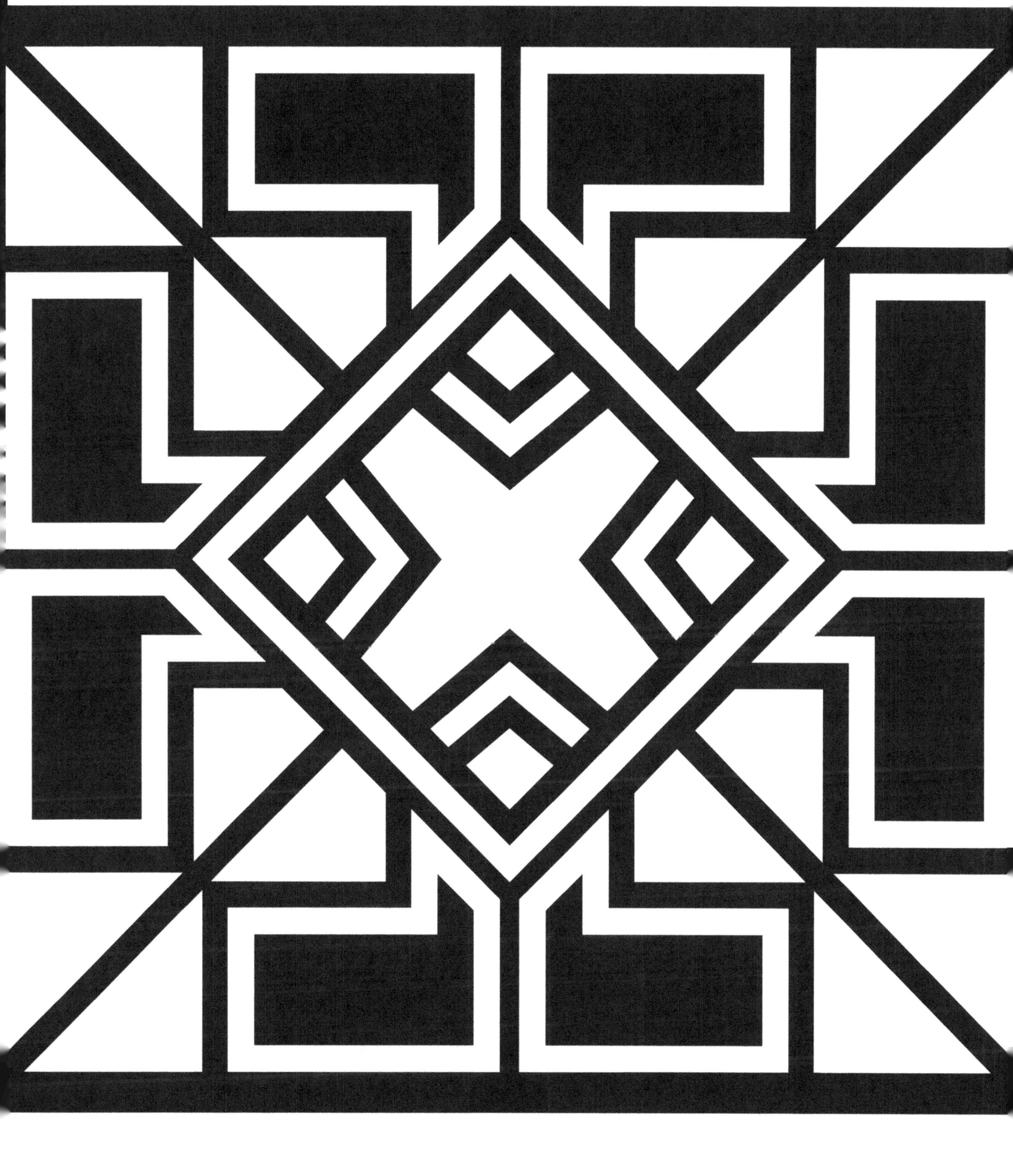

BLANK FOR BLEEDS

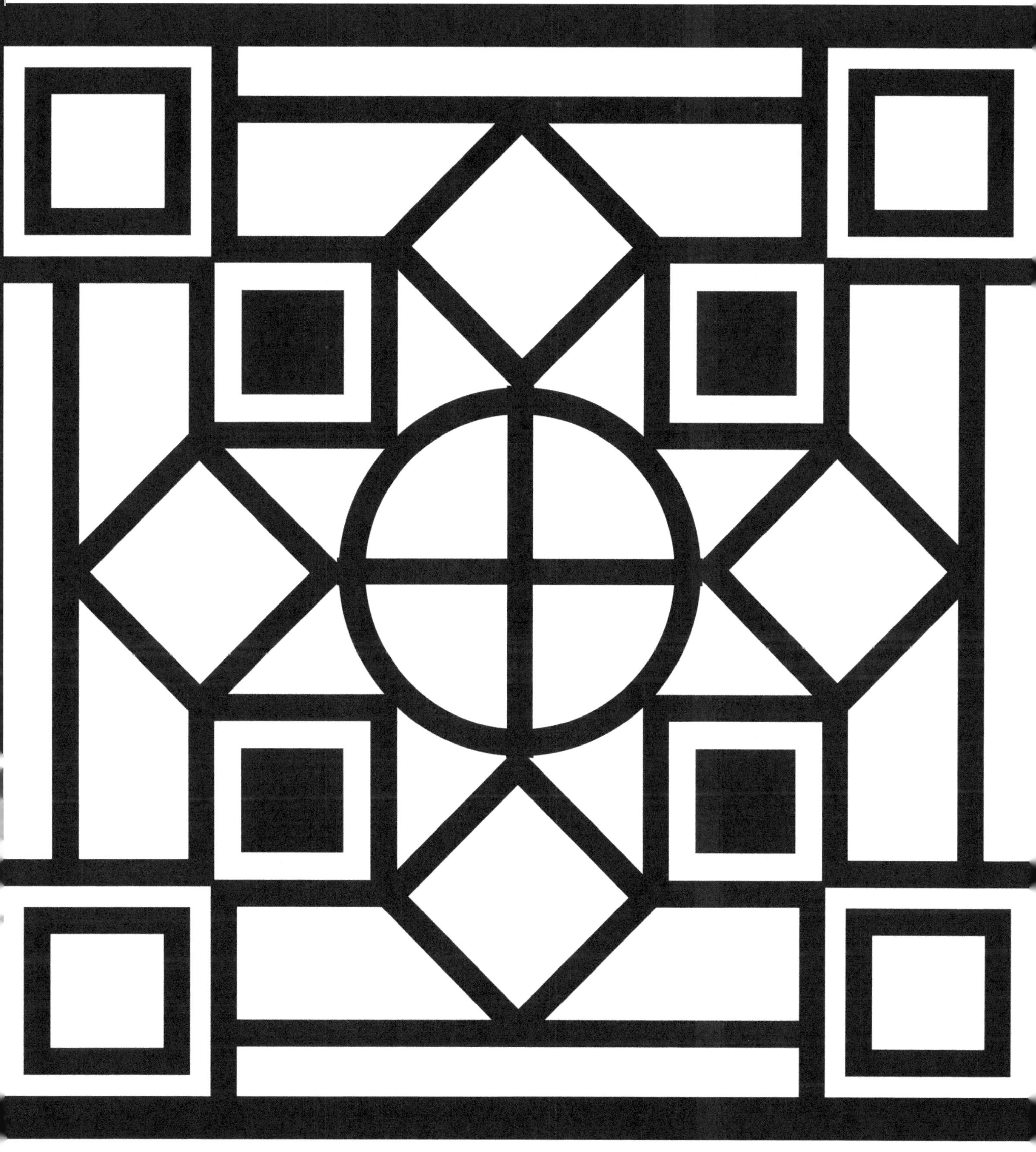

BLANK FOR BLEEDS

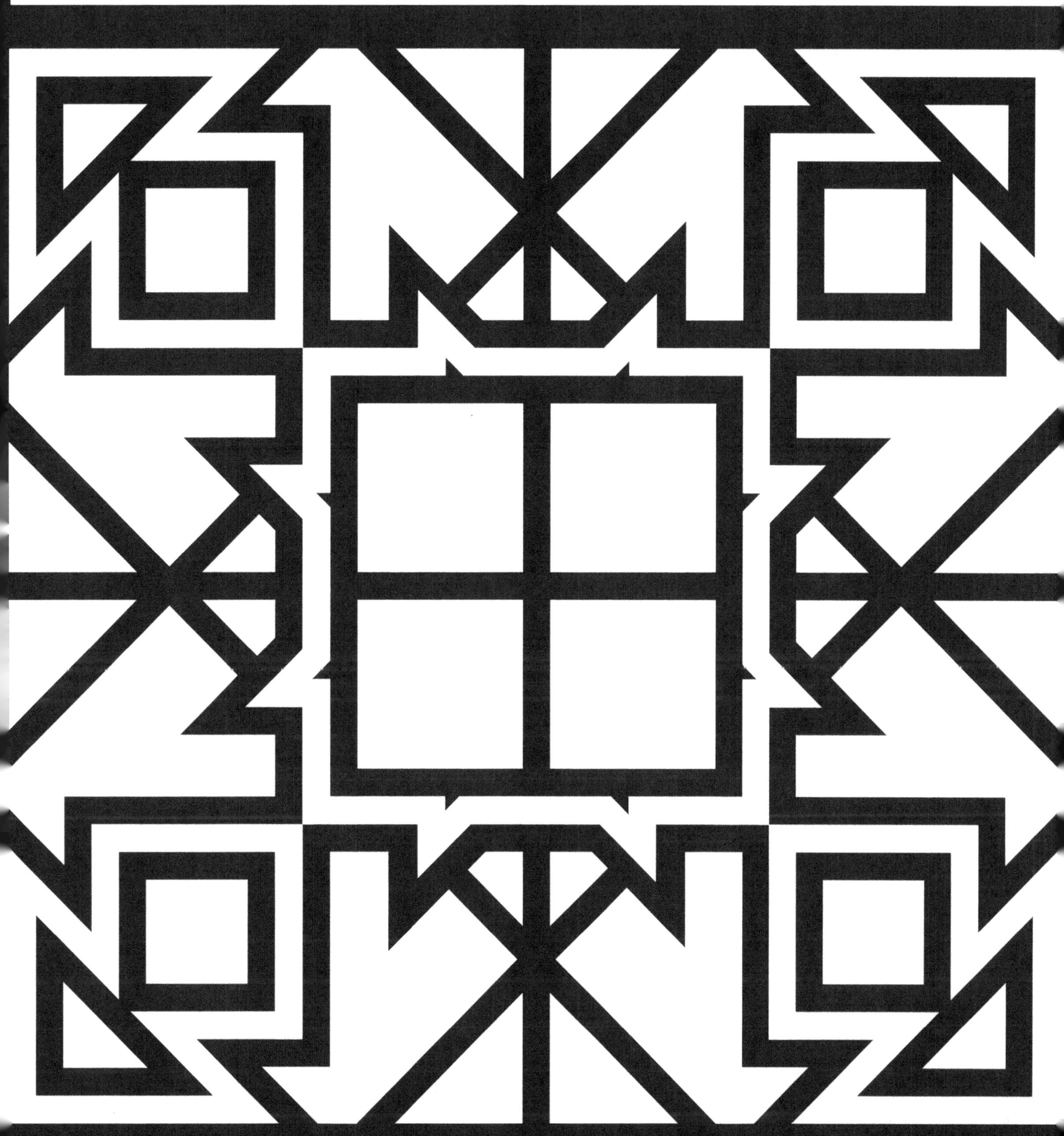

BLANK FOR BLEEDS

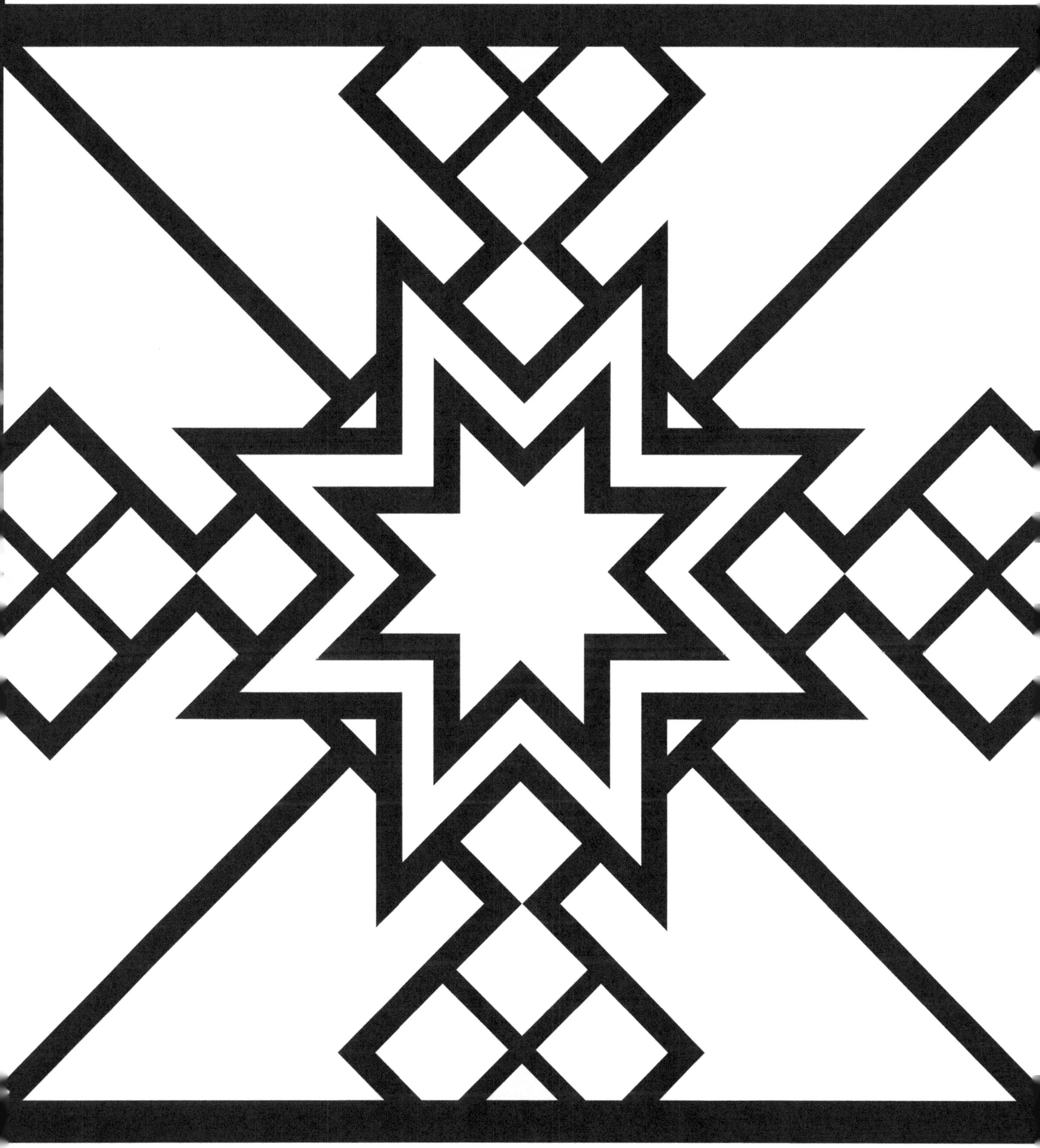

BLANK FOR BLEEDS

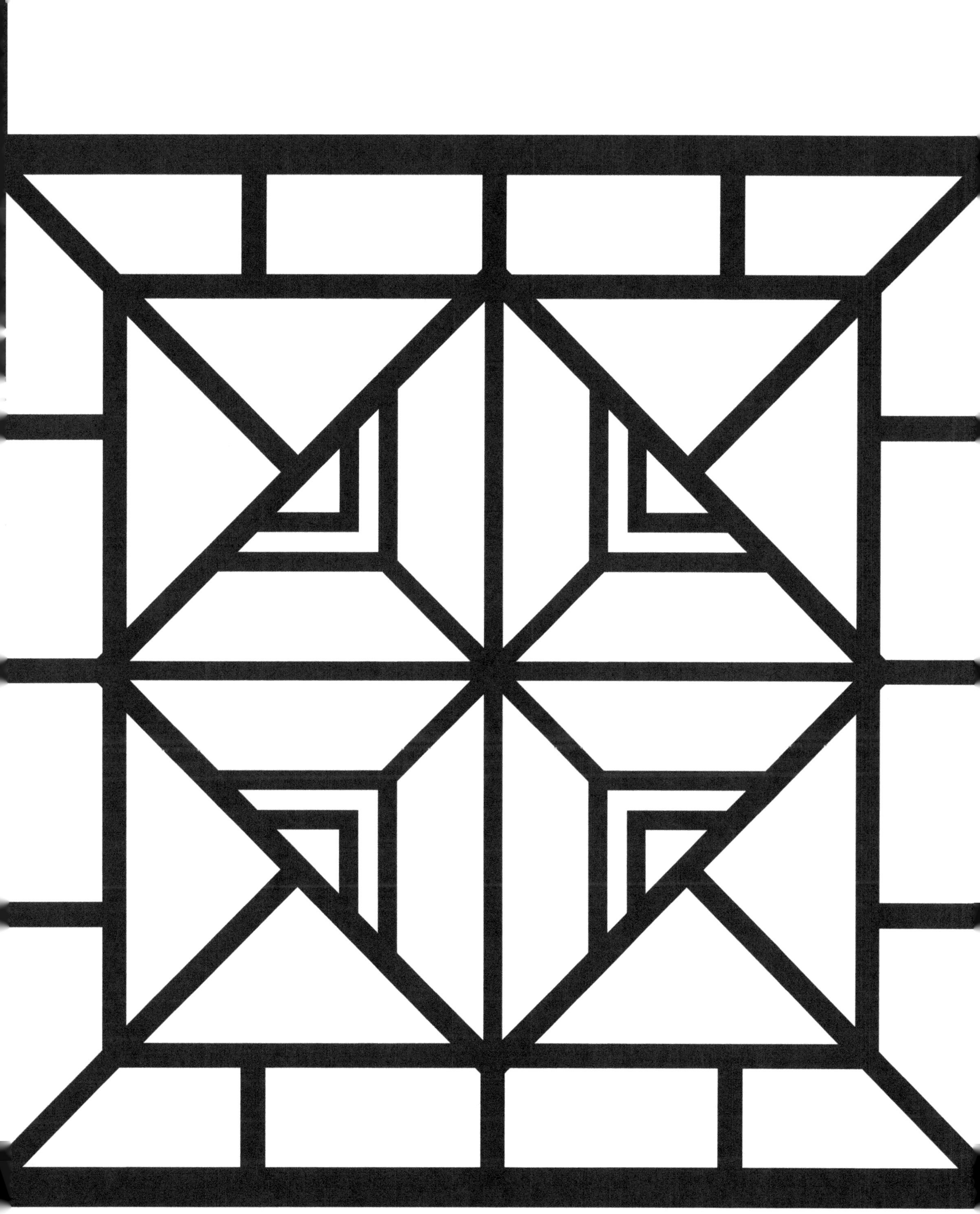

BLANK FOR BLEEDS

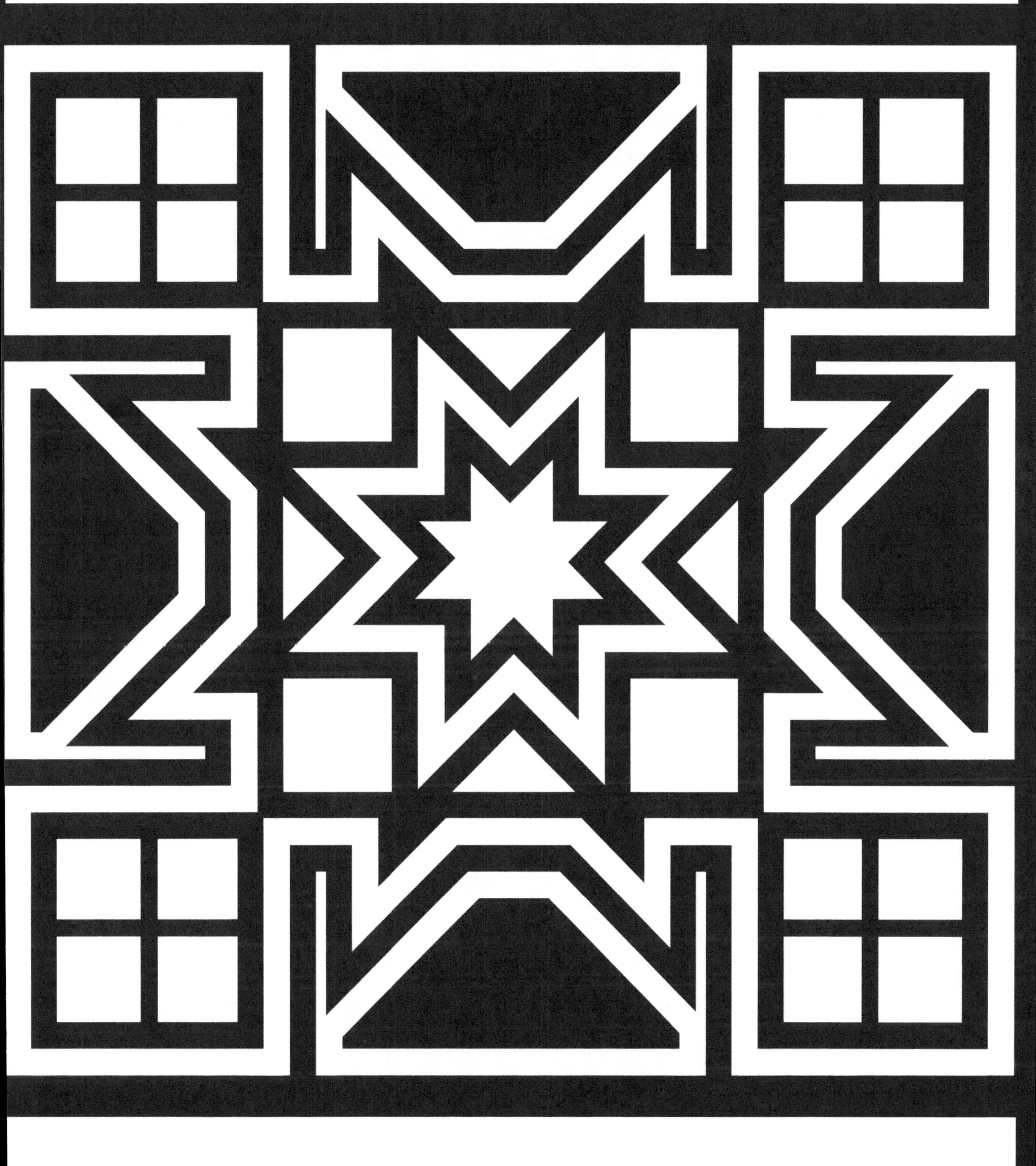

BLANK FOR BLEEDS

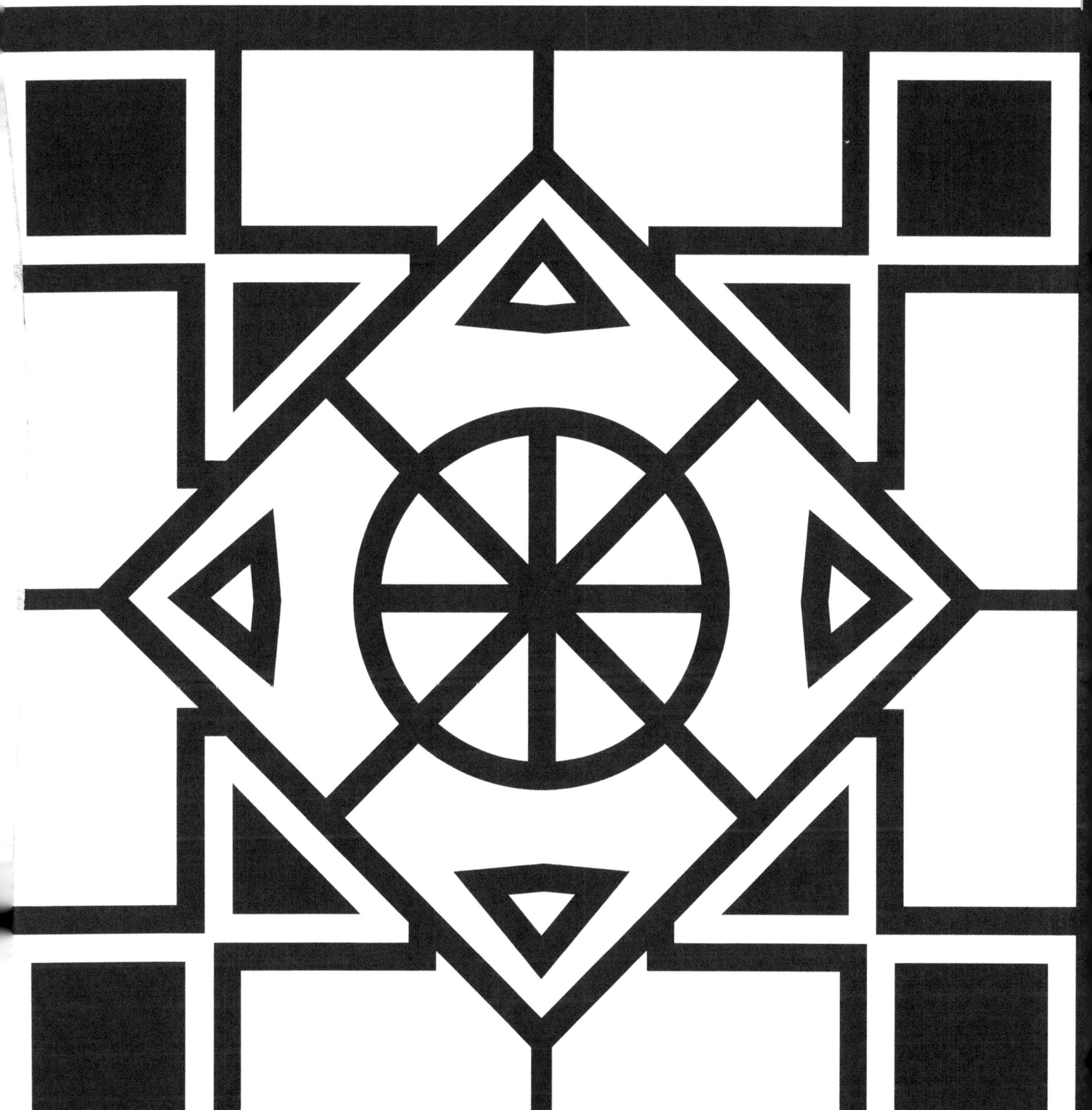

BLANK FOR BLEEDS